**ghost world**

**a collection of poems**

**by Rebecca Routh-Sample**

Other books by Rebecca Routh-Sample

*Fiction*

Diary Of A Teenage Fangirl

Diary Of A Teenage Rebel Girl

*Poetry*

ghost world

donnie darko

paramour

Spinner's End

The Greatest Love Story Never Told

All available to purchase on www.lulu.com

Connect with me on social media if you want! I'd love to hear your feedback:

Twitter: @itsbeccafy

Instagram: @beccafyofficial

TikTok: @itsbeccafy

Check out Amy's artwork:

Instagram: @amyleylaart

And buy her prints on Etsy:

www.etsy.com/uk/shop/PetrichorCorner

**contents**

1. i'm not regina george.

2. ghost world

3. i may destroy you

4. to cloud, forever sephiroth.

5. sarah lynn // the view from halfway down

6. earthbound

7. home again

8. chrysanthemums

9. ego death

10. remains of the day

11. false idles

12. fade to black

13. lavender

14. arrow

15. john ambrose

16. yeah, that's me.

17. i'll follow you into the dark

18. i don't forget

19. honeytrap

20. looking for alaska

21. queen of hearts

22. november

23. wonder

24. ashtray.

**i'm not regina george.**

just because you know someone's perception of me,

doesn't mean you know me.

you don't know me,

because i don't even know myself.

and i could tell you some things

about those friends of yours,

but this isn't my burn book

and i'm not regina george.

i'm the cocaine method actor

i'm slyvia plath's honey

i'm the person who makes you

cry

by telling a story that's really funny

i'm the palm tree that bends

but becomes stronger every time

i'm the best damn sim

in god's grand design

i'm in pain that flares like the hills in california

i'm the girl that's far too much

and takes a single look

to know that i adore you.

i'm the biggest bitch you've met

and also the best, best friend

and if you can't remember

just let me write it down

i'm not going anywhere

so you may as well sit down.

**ghost world**

living a ghost world

selfies hang around like posters

myself reflected in a hall of mirrors

refracting the best of my life

against the worst stabbing pain of a knife

that tells me to like and follow

and never give in

what if i unlike

 and unfollow

life and look within

instead of drowning

deeper

into nothingness and code

i'm 24 feeling dreadfully old

i'm just a girl

living in a ghost world

this isn't even fun

so i'll go on the run


**i may destroy you**


i may destroy you

i may destroy me

i may destroy the idea of

everything i'll never be

you took my life by

a thread

cut it like string

took a gorgeous butterfly

and clipped her wings

in london

the wonderland of possibilities

freedom, love, oblivion

on a line you try to cross

so cunningly and maliciously

you won't lose your job

you'll get a book deal with the big boss

who knows the noughts and crosses

but i care about your thoughts

a human being triumphant

in the face

of a colonialist, emotionally impoverished capitalist state

and you pulled

out her guts in the kitchen light

and you knew was going to be alright

but i care about the girl

on july 19th

**to cloud, forever sephiroth.**

satellites are falling

and dirigibles

and i'm so un-original

casting spells

and swimming pools

sitting in jumpers when it's cool

dye my hair blonde

and play the fool

forget what i learned in school

like how to love somebody

until you rip up every inch of you

and duct tape

your mouth shut


so no one has to hear your whining

and every taunt sewn into your skin

just like a human diary

and drown so deep you never ever stop

to cloud, forever sephiroth.

**sarah lynn // the view from halfway down**

sarah lynn,

where have you been and where you going?

sarah lynn,

have you ever stared into the abyss unknowing?

the view from halfway down

doesn't look so good now

why would you go

when so many people want you around?

i'm so sorry your tears burn your eyes

i'm so sorry that all the vultures just tell lies

but i promise we all want you around

darling, we wish you were around


we won't hear your voice again

we won't be blinded by your light

london is lonelier

and england is colder

and we're all growing older

but not you, not you


sarah lynn,

now we know where you've been

i hope it's kinder where you're going

i hope it's nicer where you're going


but we still wish you where what we're holding.

**earthbound**

i've tried so hard

to stay alive,

i've lived so long

it's hard to try

maybe 27

is all you got

when you hate too much

and you love a lot

you pick your poison

or your cure

pick Phoenix down

or leave the party forever

and you'll never dance again

i've lived many lives

i've found it hard to try

it's just really hard

when you belong up in the sky

maybe i'm just a Starman

who fell too many times

maybe i'm lost just waiting to be found?

or maybe i'm just not earthbound?


i've tried to find a lover

who gets my many whims

through the high and the lows

and knows i'll never dip

i thought i found an angel

but they were just too high

so maybe it's not meant to be

this lifetime

maybe i'm lost just waiting to be found,

or maybe i'm just not earthbound?

maybe i'm just not earthbound

**home again**

i love you

like the sea loves the sun

like I like drinking rum

like how when I get close to

you

i run

i'm gonna ruin it all

i know it fine, well

falling dramatically and hardened

like the ground at Grenfell

the secrets I could

tell

secrets and lies

the Soap and Glory

i rub into my thighs

it burns on my lips

like our non-existent kiss

like the grass

that never touches my

fingertips

how I love you

like darkness

nooks and crannies

candle-light, folklore

and Rebekah Harkness

like the end of the day

pillow talk

hot chocolate, marshmallows

and moon-lit walks

like Connell loves Marianne

just always out of touch

slipping through my fingers

all the time

drop me a line

In the sand, in the sky

facebook messenger

a love letter through

the passage of time

time

heals all wounds

but still, fuck you

you need to ask me

'how can I make it

up to you?'

fuck you,

fuck you

again

tell me when you're

coming back

home

again

**chrysanthemums**

hollow gold and sweet surrender

you always the great pretender

holding my hand the way

i search for the holes in my sweater

it was awesome

but we lost it

what did it cost? it

broke me like honeycomb

blocked your number on my phone

erased you from my existence

obliviate your insistence

because i'm trying my best to be kind

but i can't find any anymore

so i'm gonna shut the door

because i don't need it anymore

and i ran into the spirit realm

before the ghosts tell the story

of our contradictory glory

of two people who

in order to exist

can never be around each other again

there's a road

and it has two signs

one says left and one says right

and i followed it

to castle oblivion

and i sold my soul and heart

to a demon

in this old ghost town

this ghost house

twilight and the sun down

are we even real?

or just trying to have fun now?

wrapped in ivy and chrysanthemums

in this big white room

all i wanna do

is be with you

peter piper picked a pepper

but you stole my heart

i feasted on your flesh

and i ripped your bones apart

how much longer do we have to

spend apart?

if i'm not yours

then who do i belong to?

if i'm not meant for you

then what in God's name

am i supposed to do?

i built my life around you

i built my whole damn life around you

and if it ends

i'll just be bitter

another twisted sister

cursing at the moon

writing an indie album

that ends up getting

mixed reviews

in order to know who the hell i am

first, i have to know you

i feel like i'm on the outskirts

of some grand design

where i don't have to cry myself

to sleep every night

where writers write

poets sings

actor acts

and models bring

the inspiration to launch a

thousands ships

because every muse needs an artist

and you're my mine, baby

every single time

you're mine


**ego death**


the death of all that is good

and natural

what is real

what do we feel

what do we think

and what is factual?

guilt

in waves

anxiety

in spades

fear

we're trained

to feel

anything but pain

and our soggy membrane

left out in the rain

tending to my heart

like a

garden in a second

house in spain

hot, warm and overgrowing

lily-white and i'm just blushing

you make me feel like i could be

everything you say you see

my ego is in a graveyard

with the person i used to be

tie your fingers with mine

until we die

**remains of the day**

sometimes I pray, but

all i do is run away

and what remains of the day

is the shape of your face

are you laughing? are you crying?

is this living? is this dying?

do we only give up

when we're just sick of trying

how many watercolours do i have to paint?

how many stales do i have to mate?

how many times do i have to tell somebody right before i run away?

are you my soulmate?

or just a blind date?

that i politely tell i hate

by staring out the window

at the bookshop across the street

shakes hands, nice to meet

an inconsequential person

with eyes full of defeat

and i'm feeling relief

and i go home to eat

all alone, broken bones

single bed, no need for house phones

hover above the city like a drone

like i'm too damn entitled

to say it's my my home

deliberately spill wine

on the passenger seat

i bleed out, fibroids

i'm sick, typhoid

sometimes i can't feel a thing

freeze up like an android

took a bite of the apple

forbidden fruit

etched my name

into your skin

and your dad's old suit

how long am i supposed to

live?

if i'm not allowed to have you

but i see you on tv

i see you in every single street

in every person i meet

at the altar where i put

my feet

judge me all you want

i'm a joker, yours to taunt

i'm wedding bells, rice

and microwave meals

i don't give a shit how you feel

'til death do us part

miseries of the heart

which remains do you want today?

**false idles**

who'd have known

our days would be the last

a golden light

an empty pool, where i drown

the sweetest emptiest nothings

entropy ran through

i think of something funny

but i can't text you

it's raining but it's doesn't rain

where you are

watching harry potter, alone

in a darkened room

kid cudi in the car

back then the only thing i ever

knew is that i'd known you

should have known

you were trouble when you walked

in

your exes were blonde artists

that had a penchant

for the clinically insane

i grew up on you but i was

only a child

idealistic and deluded, like an only child

and when i grew up i realised

that it is madness not genius

makes someone that wild

it was a beautiful, crazy,

distant thing

it was like the sunrise and

the light it brings

it was the man i saw on

the posters on my wall

on the DVD cover

your brand deal i saw at the mall

the headlines bring

a sickly feeling

and the videos make me weep

i listen to your music

but your stolen lullabies

don't make me feel a

fucking thing

and you don't know my name

because you never bothered to ask

when you get that fucking big

there's no one you need to thank

your day in the sun will

dim by nightfall

and your star will burn

till in implodes in on itself

playboy cover burning

in the bonfires of hell

lesson learned

don't trust a man

that would write that on their face

don't trust anyone

who has something to fake

sometimes its too good to be true

sometimes it really ain't

laser removal can only remove the ink

the scars are so deep

like the depths that they sink

baby girl, you deserve better than

that

your light shines too bright

to let someone put it out

when you say 'i love'

follow that with your own name

because worshiping false idles

only causes pain

**fade to black**

trauma is an understatement

i am still an adolescent

trapped in the same trauma

of a fifteen year old

who didn't expect anything

forced to live in a room

that smelled of death

grandad's clothes hanging in

the wardrobe

every nightmare, a regret

and she never thought she'd

make it out alive

to she runs as fast as she can

she wallpapers over the mould

she laughs before she chokes

she leaves you

before you can leave her

she dropped out of the race

so no one can beat her

she stays inside

she always lies

so if you hate her

it's just the persona

of a traumatised teenager

waiting in the cold

she can't get in the robot

with her demons on her back

she can't save the world

if they don't love her back

she crawls back into the womb

but what fun is that?

she stops breathing

the night fades to black



**lavender**


i'll see you one day

i'll see your face

every cloud is a beautiful

silver lining

each feather a gift

sea glass refracting

all your promises

i thought i'd get to say

goodbye

before you left

i thought i'd have more

time

but you can't outrun

death

i thought i'd have a

birthday card

and the inscription would

help me make sense

but i have all your things

in my bedroom drawer

and it smells like you

lavender and violet

oh how i miss you

i'll see you again

not anytime soon

but i'll see you again

i hope you're proud of me

i wish i could have one more day

i dyed my hair

and put my make-up on

and stared up at the blue sky

i planted flowers in the garden

remember the willow tree?

flossy hid under there

back when it was sunny

and the rays melted under my skin

there were butterflies and bees

oh, i wish you could see

the three of us

are doing our best to be happy

it's hard, but we're trying


**arrow**


mystic is the messenger

and frugal is the fool

that thinks you get

nothing out of someone adoring you

entropy is envious

of the energy released

by two souls intertwining


pink, purple, then blue

in every single lifetime

i'll trade my life for you

equivalent exchange

generous and giving

til the scorpion stings you


so pull back your arrow

and make sure it's aiming

away from you

**john ambrose**

i'm not enough for you

i'm not enough for anyone

i'm the problem

i'm the puzzle piece

with the jagged edge

fair weather friends

and lover's lament

i tell in confidence

to a crowd cheering

but not hearing

a damn thing

i go home alone

sit on my throne made of bones

and every blocked number i have in my phone

because i ghost you

the moment you get close

letters i never sent

john ambrose



**yeah, that's me.**


standing on the precipice

of love and hate

with an overdrawn account

and nothing to my name

but an overdrawn account

of the night we met

with that lemon and lime

and that summer sweat

and i hold onto you

like you're my keys

and i drown with you

til i'm on my knees

and you snort a couple of

keys

still be my teenage dream

and we drown into oblivion

and you see an angel no

yeah, that's me



**i don't forget**


i'm so in love with you

it hurts my soul

to know that with you

i won't grow old

when all the other people come and go

i'll still be on my own

how can you do this to me

sitting under a cherry tree

remember the first time you

kissed me?

it was in a dream

and it'll always be

and nobody else understands

sometimes you can't always

hold their hand

sometimes life rips up your best laid plans

they expect me to find another man

they don't get it

why should you?

after all that we've been through

i don't love easily

i don't forget easily

**honeytrap**

sometimes

i think i'm fine

and then it cuts me like a knife

every day of my life

is the longest night

will you come back to me?

or will we be split by the sea

i reached for your hand

but you didn't vouch for me

i see you in my dreams

and second hand recounting

of teenage dreams

like i'm seventeen

when you were the only i thing

i thought i'd ever need

and i don't know whether

to like your posts

or beg for you to come home

or to cry myself to sleep

or try to figure out why

you

aren't with me

and if i keep writing this

i won't be able to move on

so i'm closing

my notes app

i'm a woman

not a honeytrap


**looking for alaska**

i can't

talk to you when you're like this

pushing me away

whilst playing me like a theramin

there's nowhere i haven't been

with you

all the hell you put me through


twirling, like a loop-de-loop

kiss me like forbidden fruit

strawberries and apple juice

plastic dolls and juicy fruit


known since you were 10

forever, you're my only friend

when the party ends

and everybody else has fucking left


if you don't love me why does it matter?

if my heart's on a silver platter

and our honeymoon is an un-natural disaster

and our coldest winter feels like i'm just looking for alaska

**queen of hearts**

remember that night

biggest storm on record

and you know i'm the queen

of them

guess my heart commanded it

july 5th you abandoned it

so i reprimanded it

and made it rain on all these hoes

holding your heart in a headlock

and your head in a deathlock

and the magic we had

is extinguished

like a candle that's burned too long

like an eternal flame

let's take 5

let's take love

let's not score points

i just want a hug

i'm retiring from the game

can't do it anymore

something unattainable

is just self sabotage

so at last i bow out

fold my cards

queen of hearts

**november**

early November

under the crescent moon

for you

there's not a thing i wouldn't do

precarious

on broken train tracks

you say 'i love you'

but i say 'not like that'

taste the blood its so sweet

before it runs cold

you always feel young

before you grow old


maybe we could try

to live a life un-prophesied

before the knees meet the ice

before the landing of the dice

before the dropping of the needle

before the glass meets the wine

before we're too dead

to truly be alive


oh, i guess that's what you get for being hasty

that's what you get for drinking lately

that's what you get for calling me baby

and for not settling down


that's what you get

for the world spinning round

and we'll all live another day



**wonder**


never have i ever have i ever

have i ever known somebody better

than my tattooed broken scarlet letter

with Brooklyn eyes and a Gryffindor sweater

do you remember December?

when i fell down the rabbit hole

that meant i'd never forget ya


your heart explodes in shooting stars

only shines brightest in the dark

and in my hands a flickering heart

still a child as you wander

wonder where you lost your wonder?


**ashtray.**

it ends

but that's okay.

the world has gone astray

and the lamp has burned out

and full is the

ashtray

i'll see you again

i promise i'll be okay

but the sun has set

because what remains of the day

has burned away.


like the love

like the fire

like the time

like the ashtray.


like the love

like the fire

like the time

like the ashtray.

Printed and bound by CPI Group (UK) Ltd, Croydon, CR0 4YY
26/04/2024
01005757-0002